VEGAN
One Pound Meals

PHOTOGRAPHY
DAN JONES

DESIGN
SUPERFANTASTIC

VEGAN
One Pound Meals

www.miguelbarclay.com

CONTENTS

As usual, there are no chapters in my books. Just flick through and pick something you fancy cooking. If you are after something specific, here is a helpful list of all the recipes.

WELCOME

What a couple of years it's been! It feels so long ago that I was writing my first *One Pound Meals* cookbook. Now, fast forward two years and I've written my fourth book, which has been my biggest challenge yet: applying my low cost and laid-back style to the potentially complicated and so-called expensive world of vegan cooking.

This book is aimed at anyone who wants to cook delicious, healthy vegan food on a budget. I'm on a crusade to help people understand how simple it can be to start eating a plant-based diet. And the way I've done this is by making vegan food accessible to EVERYONE, to show that no matter how big or small your shopping budget, it is possible to make easy, healthy changes to your weekly meals!

I really hope you enjoy cooking these recipes and please remember to tag me in your Instagram posts. I love seeing how you are all getting on.

THE VEGAN CHALLENGE

I'm not vegan, but like so many people over the past year I have been incorporating more and more vegan meals into my weekly routine. I feel so much healthier, and I have loads more energy as a result. There is no doubt that a vegan diet can have huge benefits for your body and we should take advantage of this to live a healthier life.

As vegan food becomes more mainstream, the demand for simple vegan recipes is increasing and people are asking lots of questions about how they can change the way they cook at home. Many people feel that there is a barrier to vegan cooking: they are intimidated by mysterious unheard-of ingredients and confused by complicated techniques and trends they see online. There is also a misconception that vegan food has to be expensive. So I totally get why a lot of people may be put off and feel like a vegan diet is out of their grasp.

Despite me saying all of this, you may still be wondering if it really is possible to eat a vegan diet on a £1 budget. Even I wondered if it was possible, which was why I decided to write this book. I've absolutely loved the challenge and I can't wait for you to get stuck into the recipes. Not only are they incredibly good for you but they are quick to make, they taste delicious and I hope that some of them become your go-to favourites!

SIMPLE INGREDIENTS

STRAIGHTFORWARD RECIPES

MOUTHWATERING MEALS

THE PRINCIPLES BEHIND
ONE POUND MEALS

My One Pound Meals style of cooking has always been focused on simple techniques with plenty of easy shortcuts, using familiar ingredients that you're already comfortable buying and preparing. I want to help you save money by inspiring you to cook from scratch and give you confidence through the recipes I create. So I've written a vegan cookbook, in my own relaxed style, with recipes that are inexpensive, straightforward and that feel familiar. These are the cornerstones of how I approach my One Pound Meals philosophy, and now I have applied them to vegan food.

I like my recipes to be friendly and welcoming; I want to encourage and nurture people to have a go. I know from experience that it can seem a little scary if you're not used to cooking from scratch, so I have written this book to be your companion and guide to cooking delicious vegan food.

INEXPENSIVE

As with all my previous books, every dish costs £1 to make, per person. So I do a lot of price analysis and savvy shopping to find the best value ingredients.

Supermarkets are fighting for our custom and competing to offer the cheapest basics like rice, potatoes, pasta and even fresh veg like tomatoes and aubergines, which you'll find throughout the book. However, if you would prefer to substitute any of the ingredients for more expensive organic versions, that is totally fine. The important thing is that all my recipes are flexible so feel free to adapt them to your own lifestyle and budget.

SIMPLE

Sticking to a £1 budget makes my recipes simple. There are fewer ingredients and therefore fewer steps. Throw in some clever shortcuts and choose ingredients that do two jobs instead of one (like the potatoes that help thicken my Potato & Sweetcorn Chowder on page 194) and that's my style of cooking at home. Undaunting, quick and easy to replicate.

FAMILIAR

There are no obscure ingredients that are only available in specialist shops in this book, for example nutritional yeast, jackfruit or meat substitutes. Just good old fresh veg and everyday ingredients available from any supermarket.

It's pretty straightforward to chop and fry an onion, or boil some pasta, and this kind of cooking forms the basis of all my recipes. I want them to be recognisable and accessible to you.

ALL RECIPES ARE FOR A SINGLE SERVING

MORE THAN ONE PERSON?

Then simply multiply the ingredients to suit you.
It is as simple as that.

BANANA PANCAKES

This is a great way to use up over-ripe bananas. They create an extra-thick and luxurious pancake batter that will give you gorgeous fluffy pancakes.

To make 4 pancakes

1 ripe banana, peeled

60g self-raising flour

100ml almond milk

1 tbsp caster sugar

Drizzle of golden syrup

To cook

Cut a few slices of the banana and set them aside for a garnish, then mash the rest of the banana in a bowl with the back of a fork, add the self-raising flour, milk and sugar and whisk with a fork to mix.

Pour a quarter of the batter into the centre of a preheated non-stick pan and cook over a medium heat for about 2 minutes until bubbles start to form on the top and the bottom is golden brown, then flip and cook the other side for about 2 minutes. Remove from the pan and repeat with the rest of the batter to create 4 pancakes in total. Serve the pancakes in a stack, topped with sliced banana and a drizzle of golden syrup.

CAPER PUTTANESCA

Using the brine from a jar of capers is what makes this dish so special. Something that would ordinarily be thrown away actually has the ability to transform this into one of my favourite pasta dishes.

To make 1 portion

2 garlic cloves, sliced

2 pinches of dried chilli flakes

200g chopped tomatoes (from a 400g tin)

Small handful of capers, plus a splash of caper brine

Small handful of pitted black olives

Handful of dried spaghetti

Olive oil

Salt and pepper

To cook

Pan-fry the garlic and a pinch of the chilli flakes in a generous glug of olive oil over a medium heat for about 3 minutes until the garlic starts to brown. Add the chopped tomatoes, capers, caper brine and olives, season to taste with salt and pepper, then simmer for about 10 minutes.

Meanwhile, bring a pan of salted water to the boil and cook the spaghetti until al dente.

Use tongs to transfer the spaghetti to the sauce, along with a couple of tablespoons of the cooking water, and mix it all together. Sprinkle with the remaining pinch of chilli flakes and drizzle with a glug of olive oil to serve.

CURRIED MINI CAULIFLOWER

I know mini cauliflowers aren't as economical as big ones, but for a special occasion they look stunning cooked as individual portions and the dish still comes in under £1.

To make 1 portion

150g passata

2 tsp curry powder

Splash of coconut milk

1 mini cauliflower

Sprinkle of flaked almonds

½ spring onion, sliced

Olive oil

Salt and pepper

To cook

Preheat your oven to 190°C/gas mark 5.

Pour the passata into a small ovenproof dish and stir in 1 teaspoon of the curry powder, the coconut milk and a pinch each of salt and pepper, then place the cauliflower in the centre.

Mix the remaining teaspoon of curry powder and a pinch of salt with a glug of olive oil and brush it over the surface of the cauliflower. Roast in the oven for about 25 minutes, or until the cauliflower is cooked through, then remove from the oven, garnish with the flaked almonds and spring onion and serve.

SWEET POTATO KATSU CURRY

You could technically use any vegetable here, but I find that sweet potato works perfectly with the light and crispy tempura batter to make the perfect vegan Katsu Curry.

To make 1 portion

½ mug of basmati rice

1 mug of water, plus 150ml cold water for the batter

100g self-raising flour

4 x 1cm-thick slices of sweet potato

1 tsp plain flour

1 tsp curry powder

5 tsp golden syrup

Soy sauce

1 spring onion, sliced lengthways

Vegetable oil

Salt

To cook

Put the rice and the mug of water in a saucepan with a pinch of salt, and cook over a medium heat with the lid on for about 7 minutes. When all the water has been absorbed and the rice is cooked, turn off the heat. Remove the lid and fluff up the rice with a fork.

Turn on the deep-fat fryer to pre-heat, or heat some vegetable oil (about 3cm deep) in a saucepan.

Whisk the self-raising flour with the 150ml water and a pinch of salt in a bowl.

Dip the slices of sweet potato into the batter then fry them in the oil for about 10 minutes until golden and crisp and cooked all the way through. Remove with a slotted spoon and drain on kitchen paper.

To make the sauce, put a frying pan over a medium heat and add the plain flour, curry powder and golden syrup. Stir to create a paste, then start adding water little by little to create a sauce (you will probably need about 200ml in total). Finish by adding a splash of soy sauce.

Assemble the dish with the rice, sweet potato and sauce, then garnish with the spring onion.

BREAKFAST ROSTI STACK

This Rosti Stack is a great way to start the morning, with nice vibrant colours on a plate – a satisfying meal to set you up for the day ahead.

To make 1 portion

Handful of grated or julienned sweet potato

Handful of spinach

½ avocado

Pinch of dried chilli flakes (or dried chillies)

Olive oil

Salt and pepper

To cook

Preheat your oven to 190°C/gas mark 5.

Toss the grated or julienned sweet potato in a splash of olive oil, then season with salt and pepper. Assemble a rough pile of the sweet potato in the middle of a baking tray and roast in the oven for about 15 minutes, until the sweet potato is cooked and starting to turn golden brown around the edges.

Meanwhile, wilt the spinach in a hot pan (no oil needed) for a minute or so, and mash the avocado. Season the avocado with salt and pepper.

To assemble the dish, pile the spinach on a plate, put the sweet potato on top, using your hands to shape it into a neat circle, then top with the mashed avocado. Sprinkle with the chilli flakes and serve.

CARROT & FENNEL SALAD

Fennel is delicious in salads, especially when done in an Eastern style with sesame oil and soy sauce. See if you can find a bulb that still has those green fronds at the top, because they make a great garnish.

To make 1 portion

1 carrot, very thinly sliced (with a sharp knife, mandoline or potato peeler)

½ fennel, very thinly sliced (with a sharp knife, mandoline or potato peeler), fronds reserved

2 tbsp sesame oil

2 tbsp soy sauce

Pinch of sesame seeds

Pinch of poppy seeds

To prepare

Put the thinly sliced carrot and fennel in a bowl and dress it with the sesame oil and soy sauce. Top with the fennel fronds, sesame seeds and poppy seeds, and serve.

LEEK QUICHE

By using fine semolina flour, you can create a filling that holds its shape and eliminate the eggs to make one of my favourite quiches ever – a Leek Quiche.

To make 1 portion

½ sheet of shortcrust pastry

½ onion, diced

½ leek, roughly chopped

½ vegetable stock cube

½ mug of boiling water

¼ mug of semolina flour

Olive oil

Salt and pepper

To cook

Preheat your oven to 190°C/gas mark 5.

Line a small ovenproof dish about 14cm in diameter with shortcrust pastry.

Season and pan-fry the onion and leek in a splash of olive oil over a medium heat for about 5 minutes until softened. Remove about a quarter of the leek and set to one side for later. Dissolve the stock cube in the boiling water and add it to the pan along with the semolina flour. Remove from the heat and mix to create a paste. Season to taste, then fill the pastry-lined dish with the mixture.

Bake the quiche in the oven for about 30 minutes, until the pastry is cooked, adding the reserved leek to the top of the quiche for the last 5 minutes. Remove from the oven and serve.

FRIED CAULIFLOWER RICE

The cornerstones of my Chinese cuisine shortcuts are garlic, sesame oil and soy sauce. With these three ingredients, anyone can turn a few vegetables into a Friday night takeaway.

To make 1 portion

¼ cauliflower, finely chopped into rice-size pieces

Sesame oil

1 garlic clove, sliced

½ carrot, cut into matchsticks

1 spring onion, roughly chopped

Handful of frozen broad beans, shelled

Soy sauce

Pinch of sesame seeds

Salt and pepper

To cook

Season the cauliflower with salt and pepper and pan-fry it in a splash of sesame oil over a medium heat for about 5 minutes until soft and cooked through.

Meanwhile, in a separate pan over a medium heat, fry the garlic, carrot and spring onion in a splash of sesame oil for about 5 minutes until the garlic starts to brown, adding the shelled broad beans and a splash of soy sauce about halfway through.

Mix everything together in a bowl then garnish with sesame seeds and another splash of soy sauce.

CARROT & RED ONION BHAJI BURGER

My really simple bhaji recipe can be used for loads of different dishes, but I think my favourite way to serve it is to make it the star of the show in a Bhaji Burger.

To make 1 portion

½ red onion, sliced

½ carrot, cut into long, thin matchsticks

1 spring onion, cut into long strips

2 egg-cups of gram (chickpea) flour

½ egg-cup of water

1 tsp curry powder

2 lettuce leaves

1 tbsp mango chutney

1 bun

Vegetable oil

Salt and pepper

To cook

Turn on the deep-fat fryer to pre-heat, or heat some vegetable oil in a saucepan (about half-full) over a medium heat. Alternatively, heat enough oil in a deep frying pan for shallow-frying.

Combine the red onion, carrot, spring onion, gram flour, water and curry powder in a bowl and season with salt and pepper.

Using a tablespoon, dollop the batter into the hot oil and fry the bhaji for about 3 minutes (or 3 minutes on each side if shallow frying) until golden brown. Remove and drain on kitchen paper.

Assemble the Bhaji Burger with the lettuce and mango chutney in a bun, then serve.

TOFU SALAD

This Vietnamese-inspired recipe contrasts the summery flavours of mint with spicy chilli and sharp lime to create a perfectly balanced dish.

To make 1 portion

2 tbsp sesame oil

2 tbsp soy sauce

2 tbsp golden syrup

Pinch of grated ginger

Pinch of dried chilli flakes

1 garlic clove, crushed

¼ lime

100g firm tofu, cubed

½ sheet of dried vermicelli noodles

½ gem lettuce, roughly chopped

¼ carrot, cut into matchsticks

Small handful of peanuts

A few fresh mint leaves

To cook

Mix the sesame oil, soy sauce, golden syrup, grated ginger, chilli flakes, crushed garlic and the juice of the lime in a bowl. Add the tofu, stir to coat and leave it to marinate for 10 minutes while you prepare the rest of the salad.

Meanwhile, blanch the noodles briefly in boiling water, according to the packet instructions. Drain.

Mix together the drained noodles in a bowl with the chopped lettuce, carrot, peanuts and mint leaves. Add the tofu, pour over the remaining marinade, then serve.

BLACK BEAN BALLS

In this book I wanted to prove that vegan food can be homely, hearty and satisfying, and what better dish to demonstrate this than these comforting Black Bean Balls.

To make 1 portion

1 red onion, ½ finely diced, ½ sliced

200g black beans (from a 400g tin), including half the liquid from the tin

2 garlic cloves, 1 crushed, 1 sliced

2 pinches of dried oregano

1 tbsp plain flour

200g chopped tomatoes (from a 400g tin)

Olive oil

Salt and pepper

To cook

Pan-fry the finely diced red onion in a splash of olive oil over a medium heat for a few minutes, then add the black beans (plus the liquid), crushed garlic and one pinch of the oregano and season with salt and pepper. Simmer for about 7 minutes until all the liquid has evaporated, then remove from the heat and allow to cool. Mix in the flour to bring the mixture together and form it into 5 balls.

Pan-fry the Black Bean Balls in a splash of olive oil along with sliced onion and sliced garlic for about 5 minutes until the garlic starts to brown, then add the chopped tomatoes, season with salt, pepper and the remaining oregano and simmer for about 5 minutes until the sauce thickens.

BUTTERNUT QUESADILLA

To create an oozy vegan filling for my quesadilla, I decided to use gooey oven-roasted butternut squash mixed with ground cumin.

To make 1 portion

¼ butternut squash, peeled and roughly diced

1 tsp ground cumin

1 tsp smoked paprika

2 tbsp tinned black beans

1 spring onion, sliced

40g plain flour, plus extra for dusting

25ml cold water

Olive oil

Salt and pepper

To cook

Preheat your oven to 190°C/gas mark 5.

Put the squash in a roasting tray, sprinkle it with the cumin and paprika, drizzle with olive oil and toss to coat, season with salt and pepper and roast in the oven for about 30 minutes until soft. Remove from the oven, mash the butternut squash with a fork, and add the black beans and spring onion.

Meanwhile, mix the flour and water in a bowl with a pinch of salt to form a dough. Dust the worktop with a little flour, then knead the dough for a minute until smooth. Roll into a circle about 20cm in diameter.

Heat a dry frying pan over a high heat, add the tortilla and cook for about 5 seconds to set the shape of the tortilla, then spoon the filling onto one side and fold the tortilla in half. Add a splash of olive oil to the pan and cook the folded quesadilla for about 4 minutes on each side until golden brown. Remove from the heat and serve.

AUBERGINE SKEWERS

The sauce for these Asian-style Aubergine Skewers becomes extra-sticky as it bakes in the oven, becoming thick and beautifully caramelised.

To make 2 skewers

¼ aubergine, cut into 2cm squares

4 tbsp golden syrup

2 tbsp soy sauce for the marinade, 1 tsp for the dressing

2 tbsp sesame oil for the marinade, 1 tsp for the dressing

2 garlic cloves, crushed

¼ carrot, cut into matchsticks

¼ courgette, cut into thin strips with a potato peeler

Pinch of sesame seeds

To cook

Preheat your oven to 190°C/gas mark 5.

Push the aubergine squares onto two wooden skewers and lay them in an ovenproof dish.

Mix the golden syrup, soy sauce, sesame oil and crushed garlic in a bowl to create the sauce and pour it over the top of the skewers. Cook in the oven for about 30 minutes, basting the aubergine every so often with the marinade, until the sauce has reduced and become a sticky glaze that sticks to the aubergine. At this point it is ready to serve.

Combine the remaining teaspoon of soy sauce with the teaspoon of sesame oil. Dress the carrot matchsticks and courgette strips in the mixture then serve with the Aubergine Skewers and garnish with sesame seeds.

STICKY AUBERGINE BAO

This looks like quite a technical dish that needs specialist equipment, but I just stick a colander on top of a saucepan of boiling water and throw a lid on top to improvise a steamer for the buns, and it works a treat!

To make 2 bao buns

40g self-raising flour, plus extra for dusting

20ml cold water

1 tbsp golden syrup, plus 1 tsp for the bao

¼ aubergine, cut into semi-circles

Sesame oil

1 garlic clove, crushed

1 tbsp soy sauce

Pinch of sesame seeds

½ spring onion, cut into thin strips

Salt

To cook

First, improvise a steamer for cooking the bun. Grab a saucepan, fill it a quarter full of water, place a colander on top and find either a lid or a plate to sit on top of the colander (it is important that the water does not touch the base of the colander). Turn on the hob and bring the water to the boil.

Grab a bowl, add the self-raising flour, water and the teaspoon of golden syrup, along with a pinch of salt, and mix together to form a dough. Dust the worktop with a little flour, then knead the dough on the worktop for a few minutes until smooth. Roll it out to two 10 x 5cm oval shapes, then fold each one in half and squash them down slightly to create a bao bun shape. Place them on a piece of greaseproof paper and put them in the steamer, with the lid on, for 10 minutes, until they are puffed up and fluffy.

Meanwhile, pan-fry the aubergine in a splash of sesame oil over a medium heat for a couple of minutes, then add the crushed garlic, tablespoon of golden syrup and soy sauce. Reduce for a few minutes until sticky and the aubergine is cooked through.

Slice open the bao buns along the fold and fill them with the sticky aubergine, sprinkle with some sesame seeds and garnish with the spring onion.

CHERRY TOMATO GNOCCHI

Here's a surprisingly simple and satisfying sauce for you to try out. It is just made from the juices created by pan-frying cherry tomatoes with garlic, mixed with olive oil and the starchy water that the gnocchi boils in.

To make 1 portion

Small handful of cherry tomatoes, halved

1 garlic clove, sliced

Handful of shop-bought potato gnocchi

Olive oil

Salt and pepper

To cook

Pan-fry the tomatoes in a generous glug of olive oil over a medium heat along with a pinch each of salt and pepper for about 3 minutes, until the tomatoes start to break down a little, then add the garlic and fry for a further couple of minutes.

Meanwhile, cook the gnocchi in a pan of salted boiling water according to the packet instructions. Drain, reserving the cooking water.

Add the cooked gnocchi to the pan of tomato sauce, along with a couple of tablespoons of the cooking water. Stir everything together, adding a splash more olive oil and more salt and pepper if required, then serve.

VEGAN SAUSAGE ROLLS

I was really looking forward to creating a Vegan Sausage Roll for this book. It's such an iconic dish that I wanted to take my time and create the best Vegan Sausage Roll recipe ever – this is it!

To make 1 portion

½ red onion, diced

Handful of mushrooms, sliced

2 garlic cloves, sliced

1 tsp dried oregano

200g black beans (from a 400g tin), drained

1 tsp plain flour

½ sheet of ready-rolled puff pastry

Pinch of poppy seeds

Olive oil

Salt and pepper

To cook

Pan-fry the onion in a splash of olive oil over a medium heat for 3 minutes. Add the mushrooms, garlic, oregano and black beans, season with salt and pepper and continue to fry for about 5 minutes until everything is cooked and softened. Remove from the heat, transfer the mixture to a blender and pulse until you get a coarse paste. Tip into a bowl, stir in 1 teaspoon of flour to help the mixture thicken, then allow to cool.

Preheat your oven to 190°C/gas mark 5.

Cut the puff pastry into 3 strips approximately 4 x 10cm, spoon in a dollop of filling halfway along the strip and wrap to create your sausage rolls, finishing by squashing the end with the back of a fork. On a lined baking sheet sprinkle each roll with poppy seeds and bake in the oven for about 20 minutes, or until the pastry is golden brown.

ARTICHOKE PAELLA

You can pick up jars of artichoke hearts in the supermarket. I always think they feel a bit special and exotic, so make the perfect star ingredient for creating a stunning vegan paella.

To make 1 portion

½ onion, diced

1 garlic clove, sliced

½ red pepper, roughly sliced

Handful of arborio rice

Pinch of turmeric

Kettle of boiling water

½ vegetable stock cube

Small handful of frozen peas

A few pieces of artichoke heart from a jar

Olive oil

Salt and pepper

To cook

Pan-fry the onion in a splash of olive oil over a medium heat for a few minutes until softened, then add the garlic and fry for a few more minutes. Just before the garlic starts to brown, add the red pepper, arborio rice and turmeric, and season with salt and pepper. Stir for 1 minute to coat the rice in the oil and turmeric, then add 100ml of the boiling water and crumble in the stock cube. Stir continuously while the water simmers and gets absorbed by the rice, gradually adding more water (100ml at a time – you will need about 400ml in total), until the rice is tender and cooked – it should take about 15 minutes.

When the rice is cooked, stir in the frozen peas and cook for about 3 minutes, then stir in the pieces of artichoke. Remove from the heat, season to taste and serve.

LASAGNE SOUP

I thought it would be quite cool to use lasagne sheets in a soup – a sort of lasagne crossed with a minestrone soup – and it worked!

To make 1 portion

½ onion, sliced

200g cannellini beans (from a 400g tin), drained

200g chopped tomatoes (from a 400g tin)

Pinch of dried oregano

½ vegetable stock cube

2 dried lasagne sheets

Handful of kale

Salt and pepper

To cook

Pan-fry the onion in a splash of olive oil over a medium heat for about 3 minutes. Once softened, add the beans, chopped tomatoes and oregano, crumble in the stock cube, and season with salt and pepper.

Snap the lasagne sheets into big chunks and throw them into the pan, adding a splash of water if they are not totally submerged. Add the kale too, and simmer for about 10 minutes until the pasta is cooked. Sprinkle with more black pepper, drizzle with a generous glug of olive oil, and serve.

POLENTA CHIP KEBAB

This is my special vegan version of the veggie classic – a Friday night Chip Kebab. I wanted to create the ultimate chip for this one: after a bit of experimenting, I settled on extra-crunchy polenta chips.

To make 1 portion

2 mugs of water for the polenta, plus 50ml cold water for the pita

Pinch of dried oregano

½ mug of polenta

80g self-raising flour

Small handful of sliced red cabbage

Small handful of sliced lettuce

Small handful of chopped tomatoes

Olive oil

Salt and pepper

To cook

Bring the 2 mugs of water to the boil in a saucepan, adding a pinch of salt, pepper and the oregano. Turn the heat down to medium, then slowly add the polenta while stirring with a whisk. Stir continuously for about 10 minutes until thick, then pour into a square high-sided tray or dish and leave to cool for an hour or so in the fridge.

Preheat your oven to 190°C/gas mark 5 and line a baking tray with greaseproof paper.

Once the polenta has cooled and formed a solid block, remove it from the tray and slice it into chip-shaped rectangles. Place them on the lined baking tray, drizzle with olive oil, toss to coat and cook in the oven for 25 minutes until golden brown and crunchy on the outside.

Meanwhile, mix together the flour and water in a bowl along with a pinch of salt to form a dough. Knead for 1 minute on the worktop until smooth, then shape into a rough oval about 10cm long.

Preheat a dry frying pan over a high heat and cook the pita bread in the hot pan for about 2 minutes on each side until puffed up and nicely toasted.

To serve, cut open the pita bread, fill with the cabbage, lettuce and tomatoes (or your favourite salad ingredients) and the polenta chips.

CABBAGE LEAF PARCELS

To make the perfect rice filling, I like to cook my brown rice with a stock cube. It gives the rice an extra depth of flavour and the dish a more luxurious texture.

To make 1 portion

3 Savoy cabbage leaves

½ mug of brown rice

1 mug of water

½ vegetable stock cube

½ onion, sliced

A few mushrooms, sliced

Olive oil

Salt and pepper

To cook

Preheat your oven to 190°C/gas mark 5.

Soften the cabbage leaves in a heatproof bowl of just-boiled water for 10 minutes.

Meanwhile, put the rice and water in a saucepan. Crumble in the stock cube and cook over medium heat with the lid on for about 10 minutes, until all the water has been absorbed and the rice is cooked. Turn off the heat, remove the lid and fluff up the rice with a fork.

While the rice is cooking, season and pan-fry the onion in a splash of olive oil over a medium heat for a few minutes until soft, then add the mushrooms and fry for another 5 minutes until nicely browned.

Drain the cabbage leaves. Mix the rice with the onion and mushrooms then put a third of the mixture into each cabbage leaf before wrapping the leaves around the filling. Place them in an ovenproof dish, wrapped-side down, drizzle with olive oil and season with salt and pepper, then bake in the oven for about 15 minutes. Remove from the oven and serve.

COURGETTE ROLLS

Imagine sitting down to this on a summer's day – this happy, fresh and vibrant plate of food will make you smile.

To make 1 portion

Handful of salted cashew nuts

2 handfuls of spinach

½ courgette, thinly sliced using a potato peeler

Handful of watercress

1 radish, thinly sliced

Olive oil

Salt and pepper

To cook

Grab your food processor or blender and blitz the cashews and spinach along with a splash of olive oil until blended but not completely smooth. Season to taste with salt and pepper and set to one side.

Drizzle the courgette slices with olive oil, season with salt and pepper then cook on a hot griddle pan for about 1 minute on one side, turning each slice 45 degrees halfway through to give it cross-hatch marks. Alternatively, you can just cook it in a regular frying pan.

Assemble the rolls by wrapping spoonfuls of the cashew and spinach filling in the courgette strips (with the char marks on the outside) and placing them on a bed of watercress and thinly sliced radishes.

THAI DAUPHINOISE

Coconut milk plays such an important part in Thai cooking and is a great vegan substitute for cream. This gave me an idea! I used coconut milk to make a Thai version of a classic French dauphinoise.

To make 1 portion

Handful of baby potatoes, sliced

Sesame oil

100ml coconut milk (from a 400g tin)

1 garlic clove, crushed

Pinch of dried chilli flakes (or dried chillies)

½ pak choi, sliced lengthways

Splash of soy sauce

Salt and pepper

To cook

Preheat your oven to 190°C/gas mark 5.

Arrange the potatoes in an ovenproof dish, drizzle with sesame oil, season with salt and pepper, then bake in the oven for 10 minutes.

After 10 minutes, add the coconut milk to the potatoes, along with crushed garlic and chilli flakes, and top with the pak choi. Drizzle with sesame oil and bake for another 10 minutes.

Remove from the oven and serve with a splash of soy sauce.

MAC & NO CHEESE

Butternut squash has a lovely creaminess to it, so I thought it would be perfect as a sauce for a vegan mac & cheese. I roast it to intensify the flavour and it works great!

To make 1 portion

½ butternut squash, peeled and roughly diced into 1cm chunks

75ml water

½ vegetable stock cube

Handful of dried macaroni

Olive oil

Salt and pepper

To cook

Preheat your oven to 190°C/gas mark 5.

Tip the squash chunks into a roasting tray, drizzle with olive oil, season with salt and pepper, then roast in the oven for about 30 minutes until soft and gooey.

Put the squash in a food processor with the water and stock cube and blitz until smooth, adding more water if needed, to create a thick soup consistency.

Meanwhile, bring a pan of salted water to the boil and cook the macaroni until al dente.

Drain the pasta, mix it with the butternut squash sauce, season to taste with salt and sprinkle with cracked black pepper to serve.

LAKSA

This Laska soup is spicy, creamy and refreshing all at the same time. That's what I love about Thai cuisine – it balances flavours and textures so well to create stunning, vibrant dishes.

To make 1 portion

1 tsp tomato purée

Pinch of dried chilli flakes

Sesame oil

Small wedge of white cabbage, shredded

½ carrot, cut thinly lengthways

1 spring onion, cut thinly lengthways

1 garlic clove, crushed

Small chunk of fresh ginger, grated

200ml coconut milk (from a 400ml tin)

Small handful of peanuts, crushed

Slice of lime

Splash of soy sauce

Salt and pepper

To cook

Pan-fry the tomato purée and chilli flakes in a splash of sesame oil over a medium heat for about 1 minute, then add the shredded cabbage and sliced carrot and fry for another couple of minutes. Add the spring onion, garlic and ginger, season with salt and pepper and cook for a couple more minutes until the veg has softened, then add the coconut milk (saving a little for drizzling at the end) and simmer for about 5 minutes. Pour into a bowl and top with the crushed peanuts, the slice of lime, a drizzle of the remaining coconut milk, a splash of sesame oil and a splash of soy sauce.

ROAST TOMATO TOWER

This is my favourite way to prepare cheap supermarket tomatoes – oven-roasting them with olive oil, salt, pepper and oregano. It intensifies the tomato flavour and makes them look really expensive.

To make 1 portion

A few tomatoes, halved

Pinch of dried oregano

A few baby potatoes

Small handful of spinach

Olive oil

Salt and pepper

To cook

Preheat your oven to 190°C/gas mark 5.

Put the tomato halves cut-side up on a lined baking tray, drizzle with olive oil, sprinkle with the oregano and add a pinch each of salt and pepper. Roast in the oven for about 40 minutes until shrivelled and starting to char at the edges.

Meanwhile, cook the potatoes in a pan of salted boiling water for about 10 minutes until soft and cooked through (the cooking time will depend on the size of the potatoes). Drain, put in a bowl and roughly mash them with the back of a fork. Season with salt and pepper, add a big glug of olive oil and the spinach, then mix together until the spinach has wilted. Pile the potatoes neatly in the middle of a plate (using a ring mould if you want to be extra neat), then top with the oven-roasted tomatoes and serve.

MEXICAN STUFFED PEPPERS

The sweetness of oven-roasted yellow pepper is perfect for this spicy Mexican-style couscous filling.

To make 1 portion

1 yellow pepper, halved lengthways and deseeded

Handful of tinned red kidney beans

1 tsp ground cumin

Pinch of dried chilli flakes

1 spring onion, roughly chopped

2 egg-cups of couscous

2 egg-cups of water

Olive oil

Salt and pepper

To cook

Preheat your oven to 190°C/gas mark 5.

Put the pepper halves cut-side up in a roasting tray. Drizzle them with olive oil and season with a pinch of salt, then roast in the oven for about 15 minutes until softened.

Meanwhile, pan-fry the kidney beans in a splash of olive oil over a medium heat, with the cumin and a pinch each of salt and pepper, for a few minutes until they start to pop. Add the chilli flakes and spring onion and cook for a couple more minutes, then remove from the heat and add the couscous, stirring to coat it in the cumin-infused oil. Add the water, mix together and leave for a few minutes for the couscous to plump up. Taste and season again, if required, then stuff the roasted pepper halves with the filling and serve.

POLENTA KEBABS

With One Pound Meals it's always my aim to get the very most that I can out of every single ingredient I use. Here, I've turned a humble half-mug of polenta into delicious oven-roasted kebabs.

To make 1 portion

½ mug of polenta

2 mugs of water

Pinch of dried oregano

Handful of frozen peas

½ vegetable stock cube

Olive oil

Salt and pepper

To cook

Put the polenta and water in a saucepan and bring to the boil, add the oregano, season with salt and pepper and cook, stirring continuously, for about 10 minutes until the polenta has a thick paste consistency.

Pour the polenta into a high-sided square dish, cool to room temperature then chill for a few hours until set.

Preheat your oven to 190°C/gas mark 5 and line a baking tray.

Cut the set polenta into 2.5cm cubes and push the cubes onto two wooden skewers to make kebabs. Brush them with olive oil and season with salt and pepper then bake on the lined baking tray for about 30 minutes until they start to brown.

Meanwhile, put the peas in a pan of salted boiling water, and as soon as the water returns to the boil again, remove from the heat and place half of the peas in a blender along with a couple of tablespoons of the cooking water and the stock cube (draining the remaining peas). Blend to create a purée, season to taste with salt and pepper and stir in the remaining whole peas.

Serve the peas with the Polenta Kebabs.

WHITE BEAN BALLS & MASH

The key to this dish is to get a bit of colour on the White Bean Balls by pan-frying them. This gives the balls loads of extra flavour and a nice contrasting texture.

To make 1 portion

½ onion, finely diced

1 garlic clove, crushed

200g cannellini beans (from a 400g tin)

Pinch of dried oregano

1 tbsp plain flour

1 large potato, peeled and roughly chopped

1 tbsp vegan gravy granules

Olive oil

Salt and pepper

To cook

Pan-fry the onion in a splash of olive oil over a medium heat for about 4 minutes until softened, then add the garlic and continue to fry for a further minute before adding the cannellini beans and half the liquid from the tin. Add the oregano, season with salt and pepper and simmer for about 6 minutes until all the liquid has evaporated. Remove from the heat, mash the beans with the back of a fork, mix in the plain flour and allow to cool.

Cook the chopped potato in a pan of salted boiling water for about 10 minutes until soft, then drain and mash, adding a splash of olive oil and seasoning to taste.

Once the bean mixture has cooled, roll it into balls, roughly the size of ping-pong balls and pan-fry them in a splash of olive oil over a medium heat for about 10 minutes, making sure you brown them on all sides.

Mix the gravy granules with water according to the instructions on the packet and serve the bean balls with the mashed potato and gravy.

CREAMY CAULIFLOWER TAGLIATELLE

Cooking the cauliflower two ways for this dish gives it contrasting textures and tastes, making it seem way more complicated than it actually is.

To make 1 portion

½ cauliflower, chopped into chunks

1 mug of almond milk

Handful of dried tagliatelle

Olive oil

Salt and pepper

To cook

Keep some nice-looking small cauliflower florets to one side for the topping.

Bring a pan of salted water to the boil, add the cauliflower chunks and cook for about 10 minutes until soft.

Drain the cauliflower then blitz in a food processor, along with the mug of almond milk and a generous pinch of salt and pepper, until smooth.

Meanwhile, season and pan-fry the florets in a glug of olive oil over a medium heat for about 6 minutes, and cook the pasta in a pan of salted boiling water until al dente.

Drain the pasta and mix it with the cauliflower sauce, transfer to a plate, top with the pan-fried florets, drizzle with a generous glug of olive oil, and season with salt and pepper to serve.

FARMHOUSE TOFU RICE

This quick and easy savoury rice dish is a warm and comforting recipe that highlights just how versatile tofu can be.

To make 1 portion

½ mug of brown rice

1 mug of water

½ vegetable stock cube

½ red onion, roughly diced

100g firm tofu, cubed

½ carrot, roughly diced

Small handful of pine nuts

Small handful of kale, roughly chopped

Olive oil

Salt and pepper

To cook

Put the rice and water in a saucepan, crumble in the stock cube and cook over a medium heat with the lid on for about 10 minutes, until all the water has been absorbed and the rice is cooked. Turn off the heat, remove the lid and fluff up the rice with a fork.

Meanwhile, pan-fry the onion in a splash of olive oil over a medium heat for a few minutes until softened, then add the tofu, carrot and pine nuts, season with salt and fry for a few more minutes. Next, add the kale, plenty of cracked black pepper, a splash more olive oil and fry for about 5 more minutes until cooked and the kale is slightly charred on the edges.

Mix the tofu and carrot mixture with the cooked rice and serve.

TABBOULEH

Tabbouleh is one of my favourite summer salads. I tend to use dried herbs wherever possible because they are much better value for money, but here I make an exception – only fresh parsley will do.

To make I portion

Handful of bulgur wheat

Handful of fresh parsley, roughly chopped

1 tomato, diced

¼ lemon

Olive oil

Salt and pepper

To cook

Cook the bulgur wheat in a pan of salted boiling water according to the packet instructions, then drain and allow to cool.

Mix the cooked bulgur wheat in a bowl with the chopped parsley, chopped tomato, a squeeze of lemon juice and a splash of olive oil, and season to taste with salt and pepper. Serve.

OOTHAPPAM INDIAN CRUMPETS

These Indian Crumpets are a dairy-free revelation! Rice is the secret ingredient here – it creates gorgeous crumpets with an amazing gooey texture.

To make 1 portion

1 mug of basmati rice

5 mugs of water

1 mug of self-raising flour

A few broccoli tips

A few slices of red onion

Olive oil

Salt and pepper

To cook

Put the rice and 3 mugs of the water in a saucepan, cover and cook over a medium heat for about 10 minutes, or until all the water has been absorbed and the rice is cooked, then throw it in a blender (while it's hot) along with the self-raising flour, the remaining water and a generous pinch of salt and pepper.

Heat a non-stick frying pan with a glug of olive oil over a medium heat. Dollop 1 tablespoon of the crumpet mixture into the hot pan and fry on one side for about a minute, until it starts to brown (you may need to mix a little more flour into the batter before frying, if it begins to separate). Then, gently push some of the broccoli and onion slices into the uncooked side before flipping it over and cooking it for another minute or so.

Remove from the pan and repeat with more mixture, broccoli and onion. The mixture should make 5 pancakes in total. Serve warm.

SWEET CARROT DAL

Pan-frying carrot in golden syrup creates an amazing topping for your dal – it's really easy to do and gives you a refreshing contrasting flavour to the soft, savoury lentils.

To make 1 portion

½ onion, sliced

1 garlic clove, sliced

2 tsp curry powder, plus an extra pinch

2 handful of red lentils (80g)

350ml water

½ carrot, cut into matchsticks

1 tsp golden syrup

Pinch of poppy seeds

Olive oil

Salt and pepper

To cook

Grab a small saucepan and fry the onion in a splash of olive oil over a medium heat for a few minutes until soft. Add the garlic and continue to fry for a couple of minutes until it starts to brown, then add the curry powder and the lentils, stir to coat the lentils, then add the water. Simmer gently, over a low heat, for about 15 minutes until the lentils are cooked.

Meanwhile, pan-fry the carrot matchsticks in a splash of olive oil with the golden syrup and the extra pinch of curry powder over a medium heat for about 3 minutes. Once soft and sticky, remove from the heat and use to top the dal. Scatter with the poppy seeds, season with salt and pepper and serve.

SWEET POTATO FALAFEL WRAP

You don't have to be a vegan or even a vegetarian to love falafel, but making it at home can seem a little daunting. Here's the easiest recipe you'll ever find. They're perfect for salads, wraps and even sandwiches!

To make 1 portion

1 sweet potato

1 tsp ground cumin

2 spring onions, chopped

1 tbsp sesame seeds

40g plain flour

25ml cold water

Handful of sliced red cabbage

A few tomatoes, chopped

Handful of sliced white onion

Olive oil

Salt and pepper

To cook

Preheat your oven to 190°C/gas mark 5.

Pierce the sweet potato several times with a fork and bake it in the oven for 30 minutes, or cook it in the microwave for 10 minutes, until soft. Once it's cool enough to handle, cut it in half, scoop the flesh into a bowl, season it with salt and pepper and mix in the cumin and half the spring onion. Wet your hands to stop the mixture sticking to them, then roll it into balls about the same size as a ping-pong ball. Roll the balls in the sesame seeds, place them on a baking tray, drizzle with olive oil and bake in the oven for 30 minutes.

Meanwhile, make the flatbread wrap. Mix the flour and water in a bowl with a pinch of salt to form a dough. Knead on the worktop for a few minutes until smooth, then roll it out into a 20cm diameter circle. Cook in a dry preheated pan over a high heat for about 2 minutes on each side until nicely toasted.

Assemble the wrap by topping the flatbread with the falafel and adding the red cabbage, chopped tomatoes, sliced onion and remaining spring onion.

SUN-DRIED TOMATO HUMMUS

The key to this dish is using the oil that the sun-dried tomatoes are packed in. It's got so much flavour and creates a really tasty hummus. Instead of dipping raw vegetables into it, I oven-roast them to turn a snack into a proper meal.

To make 1 portion

1 carrot, quartered lengthways

A few spring onions

200g chickpeas (from a 400g tin), drained

¼ of a 280g jar sun-dried tomatoes, plus ¼ oil from the jar

Olive oil

Salt and pepper

To cook

Preheat your oven to 190°C/gas mark 5.

Toss the carrot slices and spring onions in olive oil and season with salt and pepper. Put the carrot slices on a roasting tray and roast them in the oven for 10 minutes, then add the spring onions and roast for a further 10 minutes.

Meanwhile, grab a food processor and blend the chickpeas with the sun-dried tomatoes and the sun-dried tomato oil. Season to taste with salt and pepper then serve the hummus in a bowl, topped with the roasted veg, drizzled with olive oil and sprinkled with cracked black pepper.

AUBERGINE & CAULIFLOWER STACK

I came up with this recipe because I thought cauliflower sandwiched between slices of aubergine would look a bit like oozing cheese, and it sort of does, but the main thing is that it's delicious.

To make 1 portion

2 x 1cm-thick slices of aubergine

3 pinches of dried oregano

1cm-thick slice of cauliflower

2 tbsp passata

Olive oil

Salt and pepper

To cook

Preheat your oven to 190°C/gas mark 5.

Lay the first aubergine slice on a baking tray, sprinkle with a pinch of the oregano, and season with salt and pepper, then drizzle with olive oil. Lay the cauliflower on top and sprinkle with another pinch of oregano, season with salt and pepper, and drizzle with olive oil. Spread 1 tablespoon of the passata over the cauliflower then top with the second slice of aubergine. Top with the remaining passata and once again sprinkle over oregano, salt and pepper.

Bake in the oven for 30 minutes, or until the cauliflower is soft, then remove from the oven and serve.

BUBBLE & SQUEAK POTATOES

Bubble and squeak is a great example of a dish that was created with budget eating in mind. Here, I have added a modern twist by stuffing potato skins, using the same classic flavours.

To make 1 portion

3 medium or small potatoes

¼ Savoy cabbage, shredded

Olive oil

Salt and pepper

To cook

Preheat your oven to 190°C/gas mark 5.

Pierce the potatoes skins and cook them (skin on) in the microwave for 10 minutes or in the oven for about 35 minutes (the cooking time will depend on the size of the potatoes). Cut the cooked potatoes in half and scoop out the middles. Put the potato skins to one side.

Meanwhile, pan-fry the cabbage in a splash of olive oil over a medium heat with plenty of salt and pepper for about 4 minutes. Once the cabbage is cooked, mix in the scooped-out potato, season once more and add a big glug of olive oil. Spoon the potato filling back into the potato skins, place them on a baking tray and cook in the oven for 15–20 minutes. Remove from the oven and serve.

POTATO & NIGELLA SEED CURRY

Sometimes I just want a curry and a naan bread, but a bread that doesn't take ages to make, so I created my own naan shortcut using self-raising flour, water and nigella seeds.

To make 1 portion

1 potato, roughly diced

1 tsp curry powder

2 pinches of nigella seeds

Small handful of frozen peas

Splash of passata

Handful of spinach

20g self-raising flour

15ml cold water

Olive oil

Salt and pepper

To cook

Pan-fry the potato in a splash of olive oil over a medium heat for about 10 minutes until softened, then season with salt and pepper, add the curry powder, 1 pinch of the nigella seeds, the peas and the passata, and continue to cook for about 5 minutes until the potatoes are cooked through. Remove from the heat and add the spinach, allowing it to wilt.

Meanwhile, preheat the grill to high for the naan and line a baking tray with greaseproof paper.

Mix the self-raising flour and water in a bowl along with a pinch of salt and the remaining pinch of nigella seeds to form a wet dough. Wet your hands (so the dough doesn't stick) and shape the dough into an oval, lay it on the lined baking tray and drizzle the dough with olive oil. Cook under the hot grill for about 3 minutes until the top is golden brown and serve with the potato curry.

MUSHROOMS & POLENTA

Incorporating a few polenta recipes into your repertoire of meals is a great way to save money. It's an economical, delicious and filling ingredient. Here, it's topped with sliced mushroom and kale to make a hearty bowl of food.

To make 1 portion

½ mug of polenta

2½ mugs of water

½ vegetable stock cube

1 Portobello mushroom, sliced

1 big leaf of kale, tough stalk removed

1 tbsp vegan gravy granules

Olive oil

Salt and pepper

To cook

Add the polenta and water to a saucepan, crumble in the stock cube and bring to the boil while continuously stirring. Gently simmer for about 10 minutes while stirring, until thick, then remove from the heat and season to taste with salt and pepper.

Season the mushroom slices and pan-fry them in a splash of olive oil over a medium heat for about 5 minutes, until they are nicely coloured. Add the kale and a splash more olive oil and continue to fry for another minute or two. Remove from the heat, add a splash of water and the gravy granules and stir to create a sauce and dissolve the granules.

Serve the polenta topped with the sliced mushroom, kale and gravy.

SWEETCORN & COURGETTE FRITTERS

Brunch is served! If you're ever stuck for vegan brunch inspiration, just give these Sweetcorn & Courgette Fritters a go.

To make 1 portion

½ courgette

Handful of tinned sweetcorn, drained

2 tbsp gram flour (chickpea flour)

Handful of rocket

Olive oil

Salt and pepper

To cook

Grab a bowl and grate the courgette into it, then throw in the sweetcorn and gram flour and season with salt and pepper. Stir everything together until the mixture has a thick batter consistency.

Pan-fry dollops of the mixture in a splash of olive oil over a medium heat, for a couple of minutes on each side, until golden brown (the mixture should make about 4 fritters), then serve with some rocket leaves.

MEXICAN KIDNEY BEAN SALAD

I use kidney beans all the time to bulk out meals, but they need a bit of care and attention to get the best out of them. My favourite technique is to pan-fry them in cumin, which makes the skins split and allows the flavour to penetrate.

To make 1 portion

Handful of tinned red kidney beans, drained

1 tsp ground cumin

1 spring onion, roughly chopped

1 egg-cup of couscous

1 egg-cup of water

Small handful of tinned sweetcorn, drained

A few cherry tomatoes, quartered

Small handful of rocket

Olive oil

Salt and pepper

To cook

Pan-fry the kidney beans in a splash of olive oil over a medium heat with the cumin for a few minutes until the skins start to split. Season with salt and pepper, add the spring onion and cook for a few more minutes until softened. Remove from the heat and add the couscous, stirring to coat it in the cumin-infused oil. Add the water, stir, and leave for a few minutes for the couscous to plump up.

Season the couscous to taste then combine with the sweetcorn, cherry tomatoes and rocket in a bowl. Mix together and dress with a glug of olive oil, then serve.

THAI YELLOW CURRY

Coconut milk makes for a rich and sweet Thai curry sauce. Just flavour it with spices, add some veg, and you've got a satisfying weeknight curry in minutes.

To make 1 portion

¼ aubergine, roughly chopped

½ red onion, sliced

Sesame oil

A few baby sweetcorn

Pinch of dried chilli flakes

1 garlic clove, sliced

1 tsp curry powder

Pinch of ground turmeric

200ml coconut milk (from a 400ml tin)

Salt and pepper

To cook

Pan-fry the aubergine in a dry pan over a medium heat for a few minutes then add the red onion and a splash of sesame oil. Fry for a few more minutes to soften the onion then add the sweetcorn, chilli flakes, garlic, curry powder, turmeric, and a pinch each of salt and pepper. After a few minutes, as the garlic is starting to brown, pour in the coconut milk and simmer for about 5 minutes before serving.

TARRAGON & PEA RISOTTO

Tarragon has such a fresh summery vibe that it makes you forget that risotto normally features cheese. To get a little extra gooeyness in there, I blitz some of the peas and add them to the rice.

To make 1 portion

1 onion, sliced

Handful of arborio rice

½ vegetable stock cube

Handful of frozen peas

Big pinch of dried tarragon

Olive oil

Salt and pepper

To cook

Pan-fry the onion in a splash of olive oil over a medium heat for about 4 minutes until softened but not coloured. Boil the kettle, then add the rice to the pan and stir to coat in the oil. Fry the rice for about 30 seconds, then add about 100ml of boiling water from the kettle and crumble in the stock cube. Stir continuously until most of the water has been absorbed, and keep adding water little by little – 100ml at a time – until the rice is cooked but still firm. This should take about 20 minutes (you'll use about 700ml of water in total).

Meanwhile, cook the peas in a pan of salted boiling water. Blitz half of them in a blender with a splash of the cooking water and add them to the cooked rice (drain the remaining peas), along with a glug of olive oil, the tarragon and the rest of the peas. Serve.

PASTA FAGIOLI

This dish is a great way to use up whatever random pasta shapes you have left in the cupboard. Just throw them into this dish along with any leftover salad leaves. Here, I've used peppery cress, but it works great with rocket or spinach if that's what you have to hand.

To make 1 portion

2 garlic cloves, sliced

200g cannellini beans (from a 400g tin)

½ vegetable stock cube

Handful of dried pasta

Handful of cress

Olive oil

To cook

Pan-fry the garlic in a generous glug of olive oil over a medium heat for a minute or two. Just before the garlic starts to brown, add the cannellini beans along with a couple of tablespoons of the liquid from the tin, and crumble in the stock cube. Simmer for about 5 minutes until the beans are soft, then remove the pan from the heat.

Meanwhile, bring a pan of salted water to the boil and cook the pasta until al dente.

Drain the pasta and add it to the beans in the pan, along with the cress. Mix everything together, season to taste with salt and pepper and serve drizzled with olive oil.

MUSHROOM, SPINACH & PINE NUT WELLINGTON

This is a wellington for one, the perfect main course to make you feel special at a dinner party and best of all, it's way easier to make than it looks.

To make 1 portion

Handful of mushrooms, sliced

Handful of spinach

Handful of pine nuts

20 x 20cm square of puff pastry

Olive oil

Salt and pepper

To cook

Season the mushrooms and pan-fry them in a splash of olive oil over a medium heat for about 5 minutes until nicely coloured. Add the spinach and pine nuts and continue to fry for a minute until the spinach has wilted. Season to taste with salt and pepper and allow to cool.

Preheat your oven to 190°C/gas mark 5 and line a baking tray with greaseproof paper.

Cut out 2 circles of puff pastry about 10cm in diameter, lay one of the discs on the lined baking tray and spoon the filling into the centre, leaving a 1cm-wide rim around the edge. Lay the second disc on top and gently press the edges together to seal the filling in the middle.

Bake in the oven for about 20 minutes or until golden brown, then remove and serve.

MISO GREEN BEANS

Miso paste is a great way to add depth to a dish. Here, I use grated mushroom to absorb this intense flavour and help it stick to the beans.

To make 1 portion

Handful of green beans

A few mushrooms, grated

1 tsp brown miso paste

Handful of salted cashews

Pinch of dried chilli flakes

Splash of sesame oil

Splash of soy sauce

Salt

To cook

Cook the beans in a pan of salted boiling water until al dente.

Meanwhile, pan-fry the grated mushrooms, miso paste, cashews and chilli flakes in the sesame oil over a medium heat for a few minutes. Add the cooked beans, continue to pan-fry for another minute or two, then finish with a splash of soy sauce.

TOFU & BROCCOLI STIR-FRY

This super-quick stir-fry is spicy but also sticky and sweet, and is accompanied perfectly with a side of fluffy basmati rice.

To make 1 portion

½ mug of basmati rice

1 mug of water

A few stems of broccoli

Sesame oil

100g firm tofu, cubed

1 garlic clove, sliced

Squirt of sriracha

Splash of passata

1 tbsp golden syrup

Soy sauce

Pinch of dried chilli flakes

Pinch of sesame seeds

Salt and pepper

To cook

Put the rice and water in a saucepan and cook over a medium heat with the lid on for about 7 minutes. When all the water has been absorbed and the rice is cooked, turn off the heat, remove the lid and fluff up the rice with a fork.

Meanwhile, pan-fry the broccoli in a splash of sesame oil over a medium heat for a few minutes then add the tofu and garlic. Season with salt and pepper and cook for a few more minutes until the garlic starts to colour.

Add the sriracha, passata, golden syrup, a splash of soy sauce and the chilli flakes and cook for a further few minutes until the sauce has thickened.

Serve the tofu and broccoli with the rice, garnished with sesame seeds.

BAKED FENNEL

This recipe is almost like a fennel gratin but it uses a tomato sauce instead of cream. Baking fennel intensifies its flavour and creates a robust and hearty dish.

To make 1 portion

½ fennel, thinly sliced

200g passata

Pinch of dried oregano

A few pitted black olives

Olive oil

Salt and pepper

To cook

Preheat your oven to 190°C/gas mark 5.

Lay the thinly sliced fennel in an ovenproof dish. Cover it with the passata, season with salt, pepper and the oregano, drizzle with some olive oil and add the black olives. Bake in the oven for about 30 minutes, until bubbling and the sauce has reduced a little, then serve.

SUN-DRIED TOMATO PASTA

Sun-dried tomatoes are packed with intense flavour and they can transform a dish. Don't forget about the sun-dried tomato oil – this stuff is great, too.

To make 1 portion

125g dried spaghetti

Handful of spinach

A few sun-dried tomatoes, roughly chopped, plus oil from the jar

Handful of pine nuts

Salt and pepper

To cook

Bring a pan of salted water to the boil and cook the spaghetti until al dente, adding the spinach for the last 10 seconds. Drain, then immediately transfer the spaghetti and spinach to a bowl and mix in the sun-dried tomatoes, pine nuts and a splash of sun-dried tomato oil. Season to taste with salt and pepper, then serve.

VEGETABLE SAMOSAS

Packed lunches and snacks don't get more convenient than this. Everything is already neatly wrapped up for you in delicious, crunchy parcels with a simple but intense vegetable curry filling.

To make 1 portion (5 samosas)

¼ red onion, diced

½ potato, cut into small cubes

½ carrot, cut into small cubes

1 tsp curry powder

Small handful of frozen peas

A few sheets of filo pastry

Oil, for brushing

Olive oil

Salt and pepper

To cook

Preheat your oven to 190°C/gas mark 5.

Pan-fry the onion, potato and carrot in a splash of oil over a medium heat with some salt and pepper for a few minutes, then add the curry powder.

Meanwhile, defrost the peas in a colander under the hot tap, and when the potato is soft, stir in the peas.

Cut a long rectangular piece of filo pastry and wrap the filling in the pastry. Repeat with the rest of the filling and more rectangular pieces of pastry. Brush the samosas with oil and bake in the oven on a non-stick baking tray for about 15 minutes until golden brown.

CARROT & LENTIL STEW

Normally, thick and hearty stews take hours to cook, but using lentils and carrots instead of meat makes this recipe a huge time-saver when you need to be warmed up on a winter's evening.

To make 1 portion

½ onion, sliced

1 garlic clove, sliced

½ carrot, roughly chopped

Handful of puy lentils

200g passata

½ vegetable stock cube

200ml water

Handful of spinach

Olive oil

Salt and pepper

To cook

Pan-fry the onion in a splash of olive oil over a medium heat for a few minutes until softened, then add the garlic and carrot and fry for a few more minutes until the garlic starts to colour. Add the puy lentils and passata, crumble in the stock cube and pour in the water.

Stir and simmer for about 10 minutes, adding more water if required, until the lentils are cooked. Season with salt and pepper to taste and stir in the spinach. Once the spinach has wilted, remove from the heat and serve.

SLOPPY JOES

My favourite thing about a Sloppy Joe is the slow-cooked caramelised red onions, so I created this dish, which is overloaded with caramelised red onions then oven-baked, to intensify the flavour even more.

To make 1 portion

2 red onions, sliced

2 garlic cloves, crushed

200g chopped tomatoes (from a 400g tin)

1 part-baked baguette, cut into 2.5cm-thick slices

Pinch of dried parsley

Olive oil

Salt and pepper

To cook

Slowly pan-fry the onions in a splash of olive oil over a low-medium heat, with a pinch each of salt and pepper, for about 20 minutes, until sweet and sticky. Add half the crushed garlic and fry for another few minutes then add the chopped tomatoes and simmer for about 15 minutes until the onion and tomato mixture has a thick consistency. Season to taste with salt and pepper.

Meanwhile, preheat your oven to 190°C/gas mark 5.

Grab a small ovenproof dish or tray, add a glug of olive oil, then add half the slices of bread. Spoon the onion and tomato filling over each slice and top with the remaining slices of bread.

Mix together the remaining crushed garlic with a glug of olive oil and the parsley. Brush the top layer with the mixture then bake in the oven for 25 minutes, until the bread is golden brown. Remove from the oven and serve.

UDON MISO RAMEN

I found vacuum-packed udon noodles in the World Food aisle in my local supermarket and now I'm obsessed with them. This ramen dish looks so pretty with those pink radishes that no one would think it costs just £1 to make.

To make 1 portion

A few chestnut mushrooms

Sesame oil

2 tsp brown miso paste

Handful of vacuum-packed udon noodles

300ml water

1 radish, thinly sliced

½ spring onion, sliced

Pinch of dried chilli flakes

Soy sauce

To cook

Grab a small saucepan and start by pan-frying the mushrooms in a splash of sesame oil. Once the mushrooms have started to colour, add the miso paste and continue to fry for a minute or two, then add the udon noodles and the water and simmer for about 3 minutes until the noodles have separated. Add the sliced radish and spring onion, then sprinkle over the chilli flakes and finally mix in a generous glug of soy sauce.

TOMATO TART TATIN

What makes this dish special is the contrast in flavour between the slightly sweet roasted tomatoes and the salty chopped olives. And this recipe is actually loads easier to make than it looks.

To make 1 portion

Handful of cherry tomatoes

Handful of black olives

1 circle of puff pastry

Olive oil

Salt and pepper

To cook

Preheat your oven to 190°C/gas mark 5.

Grab a circular ovenproof dish about 10cm in diameter and squeeze in a tightly-fitting single layer of tomatoes. Drizzle with olive oil, season with salt and pepper, then roast in the oven for about 15 minutes.

Remove the dish from the oven and allow to cool slightly while you finely chop the olives and cut the circle of puff pastry slightly larger than the diameter of the dish. Apply a bit of gentle pressure to the tomatoes so that they squash onto the bottom of the dish, then sprinkle over the chopped olives.

Now grab your pastry, lay it over the top and, using a tablespoon, tuck the pastry in around the side between the tomatoes and the edge of the dish. Use a knife to prick the pastry twice in the middle (to let the steam out and stop it rising in the oven), before returning the dish to the oven for about 20 minutes, or until the pastry is golden brown.

Take it out of the oven and let it rest for 10 minutes before inverting it carefully onto a plate.

LEMONY PEAS ON TOAST

Avocados are so expensive! So, this is my alternative to the popular vegan brunch option, and it's way more interesting.

To make 1 portion

Big handful of frozen peas

½ vegetable stock cube

A few slices of ciabatta

A few thin slices of courgette, cut with a potato peeler

Pinch of dried chilli flakes

Wedge of lemon

Olive oil

Salt and pepper

To cook

Put the peas in a pan of salted boiling water, and as soon as the water returns to the boil again, remove from the heat and place half of the peas in a blender along with a couple of tablespoons of the cooking water and the stock cube (draining the remaining peas). Blend to create a purée, season to taste with salt and pepper and stir in the remaining whole peas.

Meanwhile, lightly brush the ciabatta slices with olive oil, season with salt and pepper and either griddle or toast in a dry pan over a high heat for a minute or so on each side until nicely charred.

Spoon the pea purée onto each slice and top with the thinly sliced courgette strips. Sprinkle with the chilli flakes and squeeze over some lemon juice, then serve.

BROCCOLI & BEAN CONCHIGLIE

This creamy pasta recipe uses white beans to create a thick, luxurious sauce to coat the pasta shapes (you can swap the conchiglie for another shape, if you prefer).

To make 1 portion

½ onion, sliced

1 garlic clove, sliced

200g cannellini beans (from a 400g tin)

½ vegetable stock cube

Handful of dried conchiglie

A few broccoli florets

Olive oil

Salt and pepper

To cook

Pan-fry the onion and garlic in a splash of olive oil over a medium heat for about 5 minutes until they are soft but not yet starting to colour. Add the cannellini beans, along with half the liquid from the tin, and crumble in the stock cube. Season with salt and pepper and simmer for a few minutes, adding a splash of water if it gets too dry, then transfer the mixture to a blender and blitz until smooth to create the sauce, adding more water to achieve a soup consistency.

Meanwhile, bring a pan of salted water to the boil and cook the pasta according to the instructions on the packet, throwing in the broccoli florets about halfway through.

Once cooked, drain the pasta and broccoli and mix it with the sauce. Season to taste, drizzle with olive oil and serve sprinkled with cracked black pepper.

GOLDEN SYRUP BROCCOLI NOODLES

Eating on a budget can be fun if you cook stuff that you like, and this is a great example of a dish that makes me feel really happy every time I cook it.

To make 1 portion

Sheet of dried wholewheat noodles

A few stalks of broccoli

Sesame oil

1 garlic clove, crushed

Pinch of dried chilli flakes

1 tbsp golden syrup

1 tbsp soy sauce

¼ lime

Salt and pepper

To cook

Bring a pan of salted water to the boil and cook the noodles according to the packet instructions.

Meanwhile, pan-fry the broccoli in a splash of sesame oil for a couple of minutes, then add the crushed garlic and chilli flakes. Fry for a further minute or two, then add the golden syrup, soy sauce, 1 tablespoon of sesame oil, a squeeze of lime juice, some cracked black pepper, and a tablespoon of the cooking water from the noodles. Simmer for a couple of minutes then drain the noodles, add them to the pan, stir and serve.

TURKISH PIDE

This is the Turkish version of pizza, but it's way easier to make and a lot healthier. The dough doesn't rise much, so here you roll the edges to get your crust.

To make 1 portion

40g self-raising flour, plus extra for dusting

25ml cold water

2 tbsp passata

Small handful of grated aubergine

2 pinches of ground cumin

2 pinches of paprika

Small handful of finely diced red onion

Pinch of dried chilli flakes

Olive oil

Salt and pepper

To cook

Preheat your oven to 190°C/gas mark 5 and line a baking tray with baking parchment.

Grab a bowl and mix together the flour and water along with a pinch of salt to form a dough. Dust the worktop with a little flour then knead the dough on a worktop for a minute or two until smooth. Roll it into a rough oval shape about 20cm long then place on the lined baking tray.

Using your fingertips, gently roll the edges in to create your crust. Spread the passata over the dough.

Mix the grated aubergine with a splash of olive oil, and most of the cumin and paprika, then scatter it over the top of the passata, along with the finely diced onion and chilli flakes. Season with salt and pepper, and the rest of the cumin and paprika. Drizzle with olive oil and bake in the oven for 15–20 minutes until golden brown.

LENTIL COTTAGE PIE

Lentils are a great economical substitute for meat, and provide the perfect texture for creating a homely and filling vegan Cottage Pie.

To make 1 portion

½ onion, diced

1 garlic clove, diced

½ carrot, diced

200g chopped tomatoes (from a 400g tin)

200ml water

1 tsp vegan gravy granules

Handful of puy lentils

1 large potato, roughly chopped

Olive oil

Salt and pepper

To cook

Preheat your oven to 190°C/gas mark 5.

Season and pan-fry the onion in a splash of olive oil over a medium heat for a few minutes until softened, then add the garlic and carrot and continue to fry for a few minutes until the garlic starts to brown. Add the chopped tomatoes, water, gravy granules and lentils and simmer for about 10 minutes until the lentils are cooked (adding more water if it gets too dry).

Meanwhile, cook the chopped potato in a pan of salted water for about 10 minutes until soft, then drain, season with salt and pepper and mash along with a splash of olive oil.

Season the lentil filling with salt and pepper to taste, then pour it into an ovenproof dish, top with the mashed potato and cook in the oven for about 25 minutes until the peaks of the mash turn golden brown. Remove from the oven and serve.

ROAST PARSNIP & CARROT GNOCCHI WITH PINE NUTS & SPINACH

Oven-roasting parsnips and carrots in olive oil, salt and pepper makes them so much more flavourful than if you boil them – it's little tricks like this that allow you to turn a few simple ingredients into something delicious.

To make 1 portion

1 parsnip, roughly diced

1 carrot, roughly diced

2 tbsp plain flour, plus extra for dusting

Small handful of pine nuts

Small handful of spinach

Olive oil

Salt and pepper

To cook

Preheat your oven to 190°C/gas mark 5.

Put the diced parsnip and carrot in a roasting tray, add a splash of olive oil and a pinch of salt and pepper, toss to coat and roast in the oven for about 20 minutes until softened.

Put the warm roasted vegetables and flour in a blender and blend until a dough is formed. Tip the dough out onto a floured worktop and roll it into a long sausage, then cut the sausage into individual 1cm-thick gnocchi.

Pan-fry the gnocchi and pine nuts for a few minutes in a splash of olive oil over a medium heat. When the gnocchi start to colour, throw in the spinach and continue to fry for 30 seconds until the spinach has wilted. Remove from the heat, season with salt and pepper and serve.

LEEK CROQUETTES

These Spanish-style croquettes are made with traditional British leeks and are a great example of how I mix different cooking styles and ingredients in my quest to create tasty economical meals. I hope this inspires you to give them a go.

To make 1 portion

1 large potato, peeled and cut into chunks

1 leek, finely diced

Handful of breadcrumbs

Olive oil

Salt and pepper

To cook

Cook the potato chunks in a pan of salted boiling water for about 10 minutes until soft, then drain in a colander and let the water steam off for a few minutes before mashing them.

Meanwhile, season and pan-fry the leek in a splash of olive oil over a medium heat for about 10 minutes until softened but not browned.

Mix the leek with the mashed potato, season to taste with salt and pepper and allow to cool.

Season the breadcrumbs with salt and pepper.

Once cooled, wet your hands and roll the leek and potato mash into 5 balls, then roll each ball in the seasoned breadcrumbs (the water from your hands will help the breadcrumbs to stick).

Either shallow-fry the croquettes in olive oil, turning them occasionally so they get an even colour, or – for the best results – deep-fry them in hot oil over a medium heat for about 5 minutes, until golden brown. Drain on kitchen paper, then serve.

STUFFED BUTTERNUT SQUASH

I think this is the prettiest dish in the book – I really love the colours and how delicious it looks. The subtle sweetness of the squash works perfectly with the savoury rice.

To make 1 portion

Bottom ¼ of a butternut squash, deseeded

½ mug of brown rice

1 mug of water

½ vegetable stock cube

Small handful of kale, chopped

Small handful of pine nuts

Olive oil

Salt and pepper

To cook

Preheat your oven to 190°C/gas mark 5.

Drizzle the squash with olive oil, season with salt and pepper and roast on a baking tray in the oven for 30 minutes.

Meanwhile, put the rice and water in a saucepan, crumble in the stock cube and cook over a medium heat with the lid on for about 10 minutes. When all the water has been absorbed and the rice is cooked, turn off the heat, remove the lid and fluff up the rice with a fork.

Pan-fry the kale and pine nuts in a splash of olive oil over a medium heat with a pinch of salt and plenty of cracked black pepper for about 5 minutes until the edges of the kale start to char.

Mix the cooked rice with the pine nuts and kale, stuff the roasted butternut squash with the mixture and serve.

CAULIFLOWER, CORIANDER SEED & COCONUT CURRY

Coriander seeds have this amazing lemony taste that makes this coconut curry a refreshing meal to enjoy on a hot summer's day.

To make 1 portion

½ onion, sliced

¼ cauliflower, roughly chopped

1 tsp turmeric

1 tsp curry powder

200ml coconut milk (from a 400ml tin)

Pinch of coriander seeds

½ vegetable stock cube

Pinch of flaked almonds

Olive oil

Salt and pepper

To cook

Pan-fry the onion and cauliflower in a splash of olive oil over a medium heat for about 5 minutes until the onions have softened. Season with salt and pepper, then add the turmeric, curry powder, coconut milk and coriander seeds and crumble in the stock cube. Simmer for about 8 minutes, until the cauliflower is cooked, adding a splash of water if the sauce gets too thick.

Season to taste then remove from the heat and serve with a scattering of flaked almonds.

MUSHROOM ORZO

Orzo pasta is such a versatile ingredient and features more and more in my everyday cooking. It's easy to cook and allows you to take huge shortcuts to create speedy one-pan meals – like this mushroom dish – at a moment's notice.

To make 1 portion

Handful of mushrooms, sliced

Pinch of dried oregano

Handful of dried orzo

75ml water

½ vegetable stock cube

Olive oil

Salt and pepper

To cook

Season the mushrooms and pan-fry them in a splash of olive oil with the oregano over a medium heat for about 5 minutes. Then, add a splash more oil and the orzo, letting the orzo absorb some of the oil. Add the water, crumble in the stock cube and let the orzo simmer. After about 5 minutes, once the orzo has absorbed most of the water, check to see if it is cooked (add some more water if needed and continue cooking if it's not ready).

Once the orzo is cooked, remove the pan from the heat, drizzle the dish with a glug of olive oil, sprinkle with some cracked black pepper and serve.

KIMCHI TACOS

My homemade, speedy version of kimchi is ready in minutes instead of days. It's spicy, crunchy and perfect with a bit of rice on these mini tacos.

To make 3 tacos

¼ mug of basmati rice

½ mug of water for rice, 25ml of water for the tacos

1 tbsp tomato purée

Splash of sesame oil

2 pinches of dried chilli flakes

Wedge of white cabbage, sliced

2 carrots, cut lengthways

2 spring onions, halved lengthways

Splash of rice wine vinegar

40g plain flour, plus extra for dusting

25ml cold water

Pinch of sesame seeds

Salt and pepper

To cook

Put the rice and ½ mug of water in a saucepan with a pinch of salt and cook over a medium heat with the lid on for about 7 minutes. When all the water has been absorbed and the rice is cooked, turn off the heat, remove the lid and fluff up the rice with a fork.

Meanwhile, to make the speedy kimchi, put the tomato purée in a frying pan, along with a splash of sesame oil and a pinch of the chilli flakes. Pan-fry for a minute over a medium heat then add the cabbage and the carrots. Continue to fry for a few more minutes then add the spring onions. After about 5 minutes, when the veg is cooked but still has a bit of crunch, add the rice wine vinegar, cook for another minute and season with salt and pepper. Remove from the heat.

To make the tacos, mix together the flour and water in a bowl along with a pinch of salt to form a dough. Knead for a minute on a flour-dusted worktop then divide it into 3 even-sized balls. Roll each ball into a disc about 10cm in diameter. Preheat a dry frying pan until hot, then cook the dough discs one at a time, for about 2 minutes on each side, until lightly toasted.

To assemble the tacos, put a spoonful of rice on each taco, then a spoonful of speedy kimchi, and sprinkle with the sesame seeds and remaining chilli flakes.

POTATOES ARRABBIATA

Sometimes I use baby potatoes instead of making my own gnocchi, because it's just easier. Before I serve them, I crush them slightly with the back of a fork and they almost become fluffy gnocchi, ready to absorb the flavours of the ingredients they are cooked with.

To make 1 portion

Handful of baby potatoes (skin on)

1 garlic clove, sliced

Pinch of dried chilli flakes

200g passata

Handful of spinach

Olive oil

Salt and pepper

To cook

Cook the potatoes in a pan of salted boiling water for about 10 minutes, until cooked through. Drain.

Pan-fry the sliced garlic in a splash of olive oil over a medium heat for a few minutes until it starts to brown, then add the chilli flakes, passata and cooked potatoes. Season generously with salt and pepper and simmer for about 10 minutes. Add the spinach and simmer for a further minute until wilted, then squash each potato with the back of a fork, remove from the heat and serve.

PAKORA CURRY

This simple coconut-based vegetable curry is perfect for dipping a crispy pakora into. All of the elements work so nicely together to make a well-balanced plate of food with minimal ingredients.

To make 1 portion

½ mug of basmati rice

1 mug of water (plus ½ egg-cup for the pakora)

1 carrot, ½ cut into long matchsticks, ½ diced

2 spring onions, 1 cut into strips, 1 sliced

1 garlic clove, sliced

2 tsp curry powder

1 tsp plain flour

100ml coconut milk (from a 400ml tin)

½ red onion, sliced

2 egg-cups of gram (chickpea) flour

Olive oil

Vegetable oil

Salt and pepper

To cook

Put the rice and the mug of water in a saucepan with a pinch of salt and cook over a medium heat with the lid on for about 7 minutes. When all the water has been absorbed and the rice is cooked, turn off the heat. Remove the lid and fluff up the rice with a fork.

While the rice cooks, pan-fry the diced carrot in a splash of olive oil over a medium heat for a few minutes until softened a little, then add the sliced spring onion and garlic. Season with salt and pepper and fry for a couple more minutes then add half the curry powder and the teaspoon of plain flour. Fry for a further minute then add the coconut milk and simmer for about 5 minutes (adding a splash of water if it gets too thick).

Turn on the deep-fat fryer to pre-heat, or heat some vegetable oil in a saucepan (about half-full) over a medium heat. Alternatively, heat enough oil in a deep frying pan for shallow-frying.

To make the pakora (the mixture makes about 4), combine the red onion, carrot matchsticks, spring onion strips, gram flour, ½ egg-cup of water and remaining curry powder in a bowl and season with salt and pepper. Using a dessertspoon, dollop a quarter of the batter into the hot oil and fry for about 3 minutes (or 3 minutes on each side if shallow frying) until golden brown. Remove and drain on kitchen paper.

Serve the curry and rice topped with a crispy pakora.

COURGETTE WITH PINE NUT CRUMB

I'm always looking for nice contrasting textures to create delicious and unusual vegetable dishes. Here, I've used pan-fried breadcrumbs and pine nuts to top oven-roasted courgettes.

To make 1 portion

1 courgette, halved lengthways

Handful of breadcrumbs (grated stale bread)

1 garlic clove, crushed

Small handful of pine nuts

Small handful of rocket

Olive oil

Salt and pepper

To cook

Preheat your oven to 190°C/gas mark 5.

Scoop out a little of the seeded middle of the courgette using a spoon, drizzle the courgette halves with olive oil and season with salt and pepper. Roast on a baking tray in the oven for about 15 minutes until cooked.

Meanwhile, pan-fry the breadcrumbs in a splash of olive oil over a medium heat, along with the crushed garlic, pine nuts, and a pinch each of salt and pepper. After about 5 minutes, once the breadcrumbs start to brown, remove from the heat.

Top the oven-roasted courgette with the crisp pine nut and breadcrumb mixture and serve on a bed of rocket.

RATATOUILLE

There's something honest and rustic about Ratatouille. It's not the most glamorous or intricate dish, but certainly one of the most satisfying.

To make 1 portion

1 red onion, roughly diced

1 courgette, roughly diced

200g chopped tomatoes (from a 400g tin)

½ vegetable stock cube

½ mug of boiling water

½ mug of couscous

Olive oil

Salt and pepper

To cook

Pan-fry the onion and courgette, seasoned generously with salt and pepper, in a splash of olive oil over a medium heat for about 10 minutes. Add the chopped tomatoes and simmer for another 10 minutes, then season to taste.

Meanwhile, dissolve the stock cube in the boiling water in a heatproof jug or bowl. Stir in the couscous and leave to stand for 5 minutes, then fluff up the couscous with a fork.

Serve the Ratatouille with the couscous, drizzled with a glug of olive oil and sprinkled with some cracked black pepper.

CARROT CASSOULET

Croutons might just be my favourite topping ever. Just drizzle stale bread with olive oil and they sort of fry in the oven to create an amazing crunchy topping.

To make 1 portion

1 red onion, sliced

1 garlic clove, sliced

A few mini carrots, halved lengthways

200g chopped tomatoes (from a 400g tin)

2 pinches of dried oregano

Handful of torn, stale chunks of bread

Olive oil

Salt and pepper

To cook

Preheat your oven to 190°C/gas mark 5.

Grab an ovenproof frying pan*, add the red onion and fry it in a splash of olive oil with a pinch of salt over a medium heat for about 5 minutes until soft and a little caramelised. Add the garlic and carrots and continue to fry for a minute or two until the garlic starts to brown. At this point, add the chopped tomatoes and a pinch of the oregano, season with salt and pepper and simmer for about 10 minutes until the carrots have softened (add more water if required).

Throw the chunks of bread on top, drizzle them with a generous glug of olive oil and sprinkle with salt, pepper and the remaining pinch of oregano. Cook in the oven for about 15 minutes, until the croutons are golden brown.

* If you don't have an ovenproof pan, just use your normal pan and transfer the Carrot Cassoulet to an ovenproof dish before adding the chunks of bread.

LETTUCE BURRITO BUDDHA BOWL

This lighter and fresher version of a burrito uses a lettuce leaf as a bowl.

To make 1 portion

½ mug of basmati rice

1 mug of water

Handful of tinned red kidney beans, drained

1 tsp ground cumin

A few tomatoes, roughly chopped

¼ red onion, roughly chopped

Small handful of tinned sweetcorn, drained

1 round lettuce leaf

Olive oil

Salt and pepper

To cook

Put the rice and water in a saucepan and cook over a medium heat with the lid on for about 7 minutes. When all the water has been absorbed and the rice is cooked, turn off the heat, remove the lid and fluff up the rice with a fork.

While the rice is cooking, pan-fry the kidney beans with the cumin in a splash of olive oil over a medium heat for a few minutes until they start to pop. Season with salt and pepper and set to one side.

To make the salsa, mix the tomatoes with the red onion in a bowl, season with salt and pepper and dress with a drizzle of olive oil.

Assemble the Buddha Bowl inside the lettuce leaf by adding the rice, then adding the sweetcorn, salsa and kidney beans.

AUBERGINE LARB

I've started to introduce fresh ginger into more of my £1 meals. Here, it really helps to elevate this aubergine dish into a deliciously vibrant and zingy meal, which I serve in fresh lettuce cups.

To make 1 portion

½ mug of brown rice

1 mug of water

½ red onion, diced

¼ aubergine, diced

Sesame oil

Thumb-sized piece of ginger, peeled and grated

2 pinches of dried chilli flakes

2 spring onions, sliced

Soy sauce

¼ lime

5 small lettuce leaves

Salt and pepper

To cook

Put the rice and water in a saucepan with a pinch of salt and cook over a medium heat with the lid on for about 10 minutes. When all the water has been absorbed and the rice is cooked, set to one side (with the lid on).

Pan-fry the onion and aubergine in a splash of sesame oil over a medium heat for about 7 minutes until cooked, season with salt and pepper, then add the grated ginger, a pinch of the chilli flakes, the spring onions and a splash more sesame oil, and fry for a few more minutes until the spring onion has softened.

Mix the rice with the onion and aubergine, add a splash of soy sauce and a squeeze of lime juice, then fill the lettuce cups with the mixture and serve sprinkled with another pinch of chilli flakes.

CHARRED PEPPER ORZO

The flavours of smoky paprika and charred peppers are perfect for this sticky orzo dish, so don't be afraid to burn the peppers a little more than you think you should.

To make 1 portion

½ red pepper, deseeded and cut in half

½ yellow pepper, deseeded and cut in half

A few cherry tomatoes

½ red onion, sliced

Handful of dried orzo

100ml passata

1 tsp smoked paprika

Pinch of dried chilli flakes

Olive oil

Salt and pepper

To cook

Pan-fry the pepper strips skin-side down in a dry pan over a medium heat for about 5 minutes until charred, adding the cherry tomatoes about halfway through. Season with salt and pepper, add the red onion and a splash of olive oil then fry for a few more minutes. Turn the peppers charred-side up then add the orzo, passata, paprika, chilli flakes and a splash of water. Simmer for 5–10 minutes until the orzo is cooked, stirring occasionally.

CASHEW PESTO PASTA

This is a great way to enjoy a quick and easy vegan pasta. Cashews give pesto that creaminess and savoury hit that normally comes from cheese.

To make 1 portion

Handful of dried tagliatelle

Handful of salted cashews

2 handfuls of spinach

1 garlic clove

Olive oil

Salt and pepper

To cook

Bring a large pan of salted water to the boil and cook the tagliatelle until al dente.

Meanwhile, put the cashews, spinach and garlic in a blender along with a big glug of olive oil and blitz to make a loose paste. Season with pepper.

Drain the pasta, reserving some of the pasta cooking water, then mix the cooked pasta with the cashew pesto, adding a splash of the pasta cooking water. Serve.

SPICED SQUASH GALETTE

Oven-roasted squash spiced with smoked paprika is a great filling for this galette. It's all cooked in the oven and the pastry is shop-bought so it couldn't be simpler.

To make 1 portion

¼ butternut squash, peeled and roughly chopped

1 tsp smoked paprika

25 x 25cm sheet of shortcrust pastry

Sprinkle of pine nuts

Olive oil

Salt and pepper

To cook

Preheat your oven to 190°C/gas mark 5.

Put the butternut squash in a roasting tray, coat with a generous drizzle of olive oil and sprinkle with the paprika and some salt and pepper. Roast in the oven for 25 minutes until soft. Remove the tray from the oven and squish the squash with the back of a fork.

Cut out a circle of pastry about 25cm in diameter and spoon the butternut squash mixture into the middle, leaving a 2cm-wide border around the edge. Sprinkle the pine nuts over the top and drizzle with olive oil, then fold the uncovered edges over and bake in the oven for about 25 minutes until the pastry is golden brown.

STICKY PEANUT BUTTER TOFU

I'm not sure it's possible to get any more flavour to stick to a cube of tofu than with my deliciously Sticky Peanut Tofu recipe.

To make 1 portion

½ mug of basmati rice

1 mug of water

100g firm tofu, cubed

Sesame oil

1 garlic clove, sliced

1 tbsp smooth peanut butter

1 tbsp golden syrup

Pinch of dried chilli flakes

¼ lime

1 tbsp soy sauce

Small handful of salted peanuts

To cook

Put the rice and water in a saucepan and cook over a medium heat with the lid on for about 7 minutes until all the water has been absorbed and the rice is cooked. Turn off the heat, remove the lid and fluff up the rice with a fork.

Meanwhile, pan-fry the tofu in a splash of sesame oil with the garlic over a medium heat for a few minutes then add the peanut butter, golden syrup, chilli flakes, a squeeze of lime juice and the soy sauce. Continue to fry for a couple of minutes until the sauce thickens and sticks to the tofu, then remove from the heat and serve, garnished with a sprinkle of peanuts, alongside the rice.

CABBAGE CHOP ROMESCO

This was the very first recipe I wrote for this book. I remember it felt so liberating to have a blank canvas and all these ideas for what vegan dishes I could create for £1.

To make 1 portion

1 red pepper, deseeded and roughly chopped

1 garlic clove, sliced

½ tsp smoked paprika

75g passata

2 pinches of flaked almonds

Wedge of white cabbage

Olive oil

Salt and pepper

To cook

Put the pepper and garlic in a small saucepan with a splash of olive oil over a low-medium heat. Cook gently for about 10 minutes, stirring continuously so that the pepper softens and doesn't colour. Add the paprika, passata and a pinch of the flaked almonds and season with salt and pepper. Simmer for about 5 minutes then transfer to a blender and blitz until smooth, adding a splash of water if the sauce is too thick.

Meanwhile, preheat a griddle pan or frying pan for the cabbage over a medium heat. Drizzle the cabbage with olive oil and season it with salt and pepper, then cook on the hot griddle or frying pan for about 7 minutes on each side, or until the leaves separate and the middle is cooked but still crunchy.

Serve the Cabbage Chop on a bed of the romesco sauce garnished with the remaining flaked almonds. Drizzle with olive oil and sprinkle with cracked black pepper.

VERDE

Spinach has so much moisture that if you mix it with flour it will create a dough. Just hit the button on the blender – it will look like it isn't working, but then suddenly it'll come together, trust me!

To make 1 portion

60g spinach

75g tipo '00' flour, plus extra for dusting

1 garlic clove, sliced

Handful of pine nuts

Olive oil

Salt and pepper

To cook

Put the spinach and flour, along with a pinch of salt, in a blender and blitz to form a dough. Roll it on a floured worktop into a sausage shape about 2cm thick, then use a knife to cut the sausage into 1cm-wide pieces (the pressure of the knife will squash it slightly into a longer shape).

Cook the spinach verde in a pan of salted boiling water for about 5 minutes, until they float to the surface, then drain.

Meanwhile, pan-fry the garlic and pine nuts in a splash of olive oil for a few minutes until the garlic starts to brown, then add the drained verde. Season and fry for a couple of minutes, add a splash more olive oil and serve.

COURGETTE & WHITE BEAN LASAGNE

My challenge here was to create a vegan white sauce that would form the perfect golden brown lasagne top. After a lot of experimentation, I discovered that a white-bean-based sauce did the trick.

To make 1 portion

- 1 onion, sliced
- 2 garlic cloves, sliced
- 200g cannellini beans (from a 400g tin), plus ½ the liquid from the tin
- 2 pinches of dried oregano
- 1 tsp plain flour
- ½ courgette, diced

- 200g chopped tomatoes (from a 400g tin)
- 2 dried lasagne sheets
- Small handful of grated butternut squash
- Olive oil
- Salt and pepper

To cook

To make the white sauce, pan-fry half the onion in a splash of olive oil over a medium heat for a few minutes until softened, then add half the sliced garlic and fry for a further minute. Add the cannellini beans and half the liquid from the tin. Sprinkle in one pinch of the oregano, season with salt and pepper and simmer for a few minutes until most of the water has evaporated and the beans are a bit mushy. Blitz in the blender with the flour until the mixture forms a paste and set to one side.

Pan-fry the remaining onion in a splash of olive oil over a medium heat for a few minutes until softened, then add the remaining sliced garlic and the courgette. Fry for a few more minutes, until the garlic starts to brown, then add the chopped tomatoes. Add the remaining oregano, season with salt and pepper and simmer for about 5 minutes.

Assemble the lasagne by pouring half the tomato and courgette ragu into a small ovenproof dish, place a dried lasagne sheet on top, then spread over half the white sauce. Repeat with another layer of ragu, pasta then sauce, and top with the grated butternut squash. Bake in the oven for about 30 minutes until the top is golden brown then remove from the oven and serve.

MUSHROOM GNOCCHI

I'm always looking for ways to use up leftover ingredients. Here's one for the next time you've got a bit of white wine hanging around.

To make 1 portion

Handful of shop-bought potato gnocchi

Small handful of sliced mushrooms

Pinch of dried oregano

1 garlic clove, crushed

Splash of white wine

Splash of almond milk

Olive oil

Salt and pepper

To cook

Bring a pan of salted water to the boil and cook the gnocchi according to the packet instructions.

Meanwhile, pan-fry the mushrooms in a splash of olive oil over a medium heat for about 5 minutes until golden brown, season with salt and pepper, add the oregano, crushed garlic and the cooked gnocchi and continue to fry for about 30 seconds. Add the white wine and simmer for a couple of minutes, then add the almond milk and continue to simmer for a few more minutes until it thickens a little. Season to taste with salt and pepper, if needed, then serve.

CAESAR SALAD

This is no ordinary, boring salad. Griddling the lettuce makes it a centrepiece to the dish, then everything is brought together with an amazing vegan dressing made with cashew nuts.

To make 1 portion

1 little gem lettuce, halved lengthways

2 slices of bread, cut into rough cubes

Pinch of dried oregano

Handful of salted cashews

Splash of almond milk

1 tsp Dijon mustard

¼ lemon

Olive oil

Salt and pepper

To cook

Drizzle the lettuce halves with olive oil and season with salt and pepper. Cook cut-side down in a preheated griddle pan (or frying pan) over a medium heat for about 2 minutes until they start to char, then remove from the heat and put to one side.

Meanwhile, pan-fry the bread cubes in a splash of olive oil over a medium heat, along with the oregano and some salt and pepper, for about 5 minutes. Once the croutons are golden brown, remove from the pan and put to one side.

To make the dressing, put the cashew nuts in a blender with the almond milk, Dijon mustard, lemon juice, a splash of olive oil, and a pinch each of salt and pepper and blitz until smooth.

Serve the lettuce and the croutons drizzled with the cashew dressing.

SWEET POTATO-TOPPED TAGINE

The sweet potato topping for this dish has harissa spices added to it, and it goes so well with the rich and sticky chickpea and tomato tagine beneath.

To make 1 portion

½ red onion, sliced

200g chickpeas (from a 400g tin), drained

200g chopped tomatoes (from a 400g tin)

2 tsp harissa

1 sweet potato

Olive oil

Salt and pepper

To cook

Preheat your oven to 190°C/gas mark 5.

Pan-fry the red onion in a splash of olive oil over a medium heat for a couple of minutes until softened, then add the chickpeas and chopped tomatoes, season well with salt and pepper and stir in 1 teaspoon of the harissa. Simmer for 10 minutes then transfer to a small ovenproof dish.

Meanwhile, pierce the sweet potato a few times with a knife or a fork and cook it in the microwave for 7 minutes (or the oven for 30 minutes) then leave until cool enough to handle. Cut open the sweet potato and scoop out the flesh into a bowl. Mash it with a fork, season with salt and pepper and add a glug of olive oil and the remaining teaspoon of harissa and mix.

Top your tagine with the sweet potato mash then cook in the oven for about 20 minutes until bubbling and starting to brown.

STUFFED MUSHROOM

My shortcut to traditional Stuffed Mushroom recipes is to cook the filling and the mushroom separately. This means you can guarantee it works every time and will look perfect, plus you get a lighter, crunchier filling.

To make 1 portion

1 large Portobello mushroom

¼ red onion, diced

Small handful of breadcrumbs (grated stale bread)

Small handful of pine nuts

Small handful of spinach

Olive oil

Salt and pepper

To cook

Preheat your oven to 190°C/gas mark 5.

Brush the outside of the mushroom with olive oil and season with salt and pepper, then bake in the oven on a baking tray stalk-side up for 15 minutes.

Meanwhile, pan-fry the onion in a splash of olive oil over a medium heat for about 3 minutes, then add the breadcrumbs, pine nuts and a splash more oil. Season with salt and pepper and fry for a few more minutes, until the breadcrumbs are golden brown, then add the spinach and cook for 30 seconds until wilted.

Fill the baked mushroom with the breadcrumb and pine nut filling and serve.

SINGAPORE NOODLES WITH CASHEWS

In this quick stir-fried noodle dish I slice my beans lengthways so they don't need to be boiled separately, and use cashews because I think they look a bit like prawns in a Singapore chow mein.

To make 1 portion

1 sheet of rice noodles

½ red onion, sliced

Sesame oil

1 garlic clove, sliced

Pinch of dried chilli flakes

A few green beans, halved lengthways

¼ carrot, cut into matchsticks

Small handful of salted cashew nuts

1 tsp curry powder

Soy sauce

Salt and pepper

To cook

Pre-cook or soak the rice noodles according to the packet instructions.

Meanwhile, pan-fry the onion in a splash of sesame oil over a high heat for about 30 seconds, then add the garlic and chilli flakes. Just before the garlic starts to brown, add the beans, carrot matchsticks and cashew nuts and cook for about 5 minutes, until softened. Add the curry powder and a splash of soy sauce, then mix in the drained noodles, season with salt and pepper and serve.

POTATO & SWEETCORN CHOWDER

Almond milk makes a delicious base for a soup. In this recipe, I use the potatoes to both bulk it out and also thicken it to create a filling, hearty £1 bowl of Chowder.

To make 1 portion

1 onion, diced

1 mug of almond milk

Handful of roughly chopped potatoes

Handful of tinned sweetcorn

½ vegetable stock cube

1 spring onion, sliced

Olive oil

Salt and pepper

To cook

Grab a saucepan and start by pan-frying the onion in a splash of olive oil over a medium heat for a few minutes. Just before the onion starts to colour, add the almond milk, potatoes and sweetcorn, and crumble in the stock cube. Season with salt and pepper and simmer for about 10 minutes until the potatoes are cooked, topping up with water if needed.

Transfer the chowder to a blender, keeping a few pieces of potato and sweetcorn to one side for topping the soup, and blitz the rest until smooth, adding more water or almond milk if it is too thick.

Pour the chowder into a bowl and top with the reserved potatoes and sweetcorn, the sliced spring onion, a drizzle of olive oil and sprinkle of cracked black pepper.

PERSIAN RICE

The sweet and sticky caramelised onion and aubergine mixed with plump raisins make a great topping for this easy rice dish. Just take your time and you can transform these simple ingredients into something quite special.

To make 1 portion

1 red onion, sliced

½ aubergine, diced

1 garlic clove, sliced

1 tsp ground cumin

Handful of raisins

½ mug of basmati rice

1 mug of water

Pinch of turmeric

Small handful of desiccated coconut

Olive oil

Salt and pepper

To cook

Pan-fry the onion in a splash of olive oil over a low-medium heat for about 5 minutes, until softened, then add the aubergine, garlic, cumin, raisins and season with salt and pepper. Fry gently for a further 10–15 minutes until everything is sticky, adding a splash more olive oil if needed.

Meanwhile, put the rice and water in a saucepan with a pinch of salt and the turmeric and cook over a medium heat with the lid on for about 7 minutes. When all the water has been absorbed and the rice is cooked, remove the lid, fluff up the rice with a fork, mix in the desiccated coconut and serve it on a plate, topped with the sticky onions and aubergine.

KALE SPAGHETTI AGLIO E OLIO

My favourite way to cook this dish is to fry the kale until it gets a bit crispy around the edges, before combining it with the spaghetti. Don't be scared to use plenty of olive oil – it's a key ingredient here.

To make 1 portion

Handful of dried spaghetti

3 garlic cloves, sliced

Handful of kale, chopped

Olive oil

Salt and pepper

To cook

Bring a pan of salted water to the boil and cook the spaghetti until al dente.

Meanwhile, pan-fry the garlic and kale in loads of olive oil over a medium heat for about 10 minutes, until the kale is crispy but just before the garlic starts to colour.

Transfer the spaghetti from the boiling water to the frying pan with tongs, mix and serve.

NUT ROAST

Being invited round for a Sunday roast often turns out to be a disappointment for vegans. My aim with this dish was to create something that looked so delicious that all the meat eaters would feel jealous.

To make 1 portion

1 parsnip

1 carrot

½ red onion, diced

1 garlic clove, finely diced

Small handful of cashew nuts, crushed

Pinch of mixed seeds

Small wedge of Savoy cabbage, shredded

Olive oil

Salt and pepper

To cook

Preheat your oven to 190°C/gas mark 5.

Cut a few thin slices of parsnip from the narrow end and set aside to use later on in the recipe, then roughly chop and boil the parsnip and carrot (unpeeled) in a pan of salted water for about 8 minutes until cooked through. Drain and set aside.

Meanwhile, pan-fry the diced onion in a splash of olive oil over a medium heat for a few minutes until softened, then add the garlic, season with salt and pepper and fry for a few more minutes until the garlic starts to brown.

In a bowl, mix together the cooked parsnip, carrot, onion, garlic and crushed cashew nuts, season well and roughly mash with a fork. Mould the mixture into a disc shape, using a ring mould if you have one, and place on a lined baking tray. Remove the ring and top the mixture with the mixed seeds and the small parsnip slices, drizzle with olive oil and bake in the oven for about 20 minutes.

While the Nut Roast is in the oven, pan-fry the cabbage in a splash of olive oil over a medium heat with a pinch of salt and plenty of cracked black pepper for about 5 minutes until cooked and wilted, then transfer to a plate, top with the Nut Roast and serve.

INDEX

First published in Great Britain in 2019 by Headline Home
an imprint of Headline Publishing Group

Cataloguing in Publication Data is available from the British Library

ISBN 978 1 4722 6372 8
eISBN 978 1 4722 6373 5

Commissioning Editor: Lindsey Evans
Project Editor: Kate Miles
Art Direction and Design: Superfantastic
Photography: Dan Jones
Home Economist Assistant: Sophie Garwood
Copy Editor: Laura Nickoll
Page Makeup: EM&EN
Proofreader: Ilona Jasiewicz
Indexer: Caroline Wilding

Printed and bound in Germany by Mohn Media
Colour reproduction by Alta Image
Typeset in Brandon Grotesque, Avenir, Billabong

HEADLINE PUBLISHING GROUP
An Hachette UK Company
Carmelite House
50 Victoria Embankment
London EC4Y 0DZ

www.headline.co.uk
www.hachette.co.uk